30-Day Journey

with Dietrich Bonhoeffer

classmate. Fisher introduced Bonhoeffer to the black church tradition at Abyssinian Baptist Church in Harlem and to the socially conscious preaching of pastor Adam Clayton Powell. A classically trained musician, Bonhoeffer was deeply impressed by the tradition of black spirituals, which he would later share with the seminarians he taught at a Confessing Church seminary in Finkenwalde, Germany.

In November 1931, Bonhoeffer began his duties as a lecturer in theology at the University of Berlin. He was on track to become a distinguished professor in the German academic context. But Bonhoeffer's life course was profoundly altered by the rise of Hitler and the Nazis to power in 1933. When the Nazi regime sought to "coordinate" the churches into cooperation with their ideology, Bonhoeffer helped organize the Confessing Church, comprised of Christians who resisted the infiltration of Nazi ideas and practices in the church. In 1935, Bonhoeffer was appointed director of a seminary designed to train pastors for service in the Confessing Church. Bonhoeffer led the seminary until 1937, when it was closed by order of the Gestapo.

By 1941, Bonhoeffer had been forbidden from speaking in public and from publishing his writings. He had also lost the right to teach at the University of Berlin. Nonetheless, Bonhoeffer managed to secure a post in the German military intelligence service. This ensured that he would not be conscripted as a soldier in the German military, and it afforded him a key position in a developing conspiracy to overthrow the Nazi regime. But he was not safe from the suspicions of the Nazis, and in 1943 Bonhoeffer was arrested and placed in Tegel prison in Berlin. Two years later, his name was found among those associated with a conspiracy against the Nazi regime. Hitler ordered that the conspirators be executed, and Bonhoeffer was killed in April 1945, only a few weeks before Germany was liberated by the Allied forces.

The next thirty days begin with two of Bonhoeffer's well-known pastoral books, *Discipleship* and *Life Together*, pick up a few of Bonhoeffer's shorter theological writings, and conclude with excerpts from his prison writings. Walking alongside Bonhoeffer, we will raise questions for our own faith journey. Each day's reading includes some action or thought to keep with you throughout the day. Don't merely read this book passively; actively engage with it, wrestle with what it says, and follow the recommended takeaway for each day. In reading the daily passage, consider how Bonhoeffer challenges you to commit to a new venture of faith. How might you be inspired to get out of a spiritual rut, to reach out and mend a broken relationship, or to find a new way to serve God and neighbor? I invite you to reflect on these passages as a window into the profound depths of a theologian who is rightly revered as a twentieth-century martyr. Attending to his writings for thirty days inspires and deepens our own journey of faith.

Days 1–30

Day One

Only those who in following Christ leave everything they have can stand and say that they are justified solely by grace.

We begin our journey with Bonhoeffer with several readings from *Discipleship*. Largely a commentary on Jesus's Sermon on the Mount (Matthew 5–7), this book has become a classic text of Christian ethics and spirituality. While the early English translations titled it *The Cost of Discipleship*, the original German title of *Nachfolge* means simply *discipleship*. More literally, *Nachfolge* means *following after*, so that the meaning of *discipleship* in German vividly emphasizes that disciples are those who follow after Jesus. Bonhoeffer emphasizes that disciples leave their old lives behind and follow Jesus, wherever he calls.

Reflection

The way we live in our everyday lives influences our relationship with God. While we know that salvation is a gift from God, we also know that how we live matters. We are saved by grace but also need to choose to live as disciples. Bonhoeffer talks about the importance of discipleship, of leaving everything behind to follow Jesus Christ. To be a disciple is to hear the call of Christ, follow after him, and find the salvation that is possible only as God's gift. In taking this step, we find true freedom and realize that it was God who made such a step possible in the first place. Taking that step of discipleship helps us see in time what God's grace means for our lives. What is one thing you could leave behind today as you follow Christ? Take that first step and pay attention to what unfolds in response.

Cheap grace is preaching forgiveness without repentance; it is baptism without the discipline of community; it is the Lord's Supper without confession of sin; it is absolution without personal confession. Cheap grace is grace without discipleship, grace without the cross, grace without the living, incarnate Jesus Christ.

Reflection

It can be tempting to think that because we are saved by God's grace, there is little left for us to do. Bonhoeffer calls this "cheap grace" and contrasts it with "costly grace." Confessing our sin and asking for forgiveness doesn't come easily. We crave the justified feeling of being right and avoid the shame of acknowledging where we've gone wrong and caused pain and hurt to others. Real grace—what Bonhoeffer calls costly grace—comes at a price. Without repentance and forgiveness, Bonhoeffer says, there is only cheap grace. Through confessing where we've gone wrong, we can fully experience the meaning of grace in our lives, and we can begin to repair our relationships with others and with God. Reflect on an area of your life where you need to repent and ask for forgiveness. Take on the challenge of asking for forgiveness—and forgiving others—as part of experiencing the fullness of grace.

[Costly grace] is costly, because it calls to discipleship; it is grace, because it calls us to follow Jesus Christ. It is costly, because it costs people their lives; it is grace, because it thereby makes them live. It is costly, because it condemns sin; it is grace, because it justifies the sinner. Above all, grace is costly, because it was costly to God, because it costs God the life of God's Son—"you were bought with a price"—and because nothing can be cheap to us which is costly to God. Above all, it is grace because the life of God's Son was not too costly for God to give in order to make us live. God did, indeed, give him up for us. Costly grace is the incarnation of God.

Reflection

We tend to value most highly the things for which we've paid most dearly. Whether it is a nice piece of clothing, a challenging education, or a project at work, we love things most when we can see how much work we put into obtaining them. There is something counterintuitive about this. We tend to think that getting something for free would be great—all the benefit without all the work! But on reflection we find that our gratitude and satisfaction for any achievement grow deeper in accordance with how costly it was to get from point A to point B, whether in terms of time, resources, money, or simply hard work. Bonhoeffer shows how this reality extends to our relationship with God. Cheap grace is shallow spirituality; we put nothing in and get nothing out. Costly grace means that we were bought with a price. Our salvation is deeply costly not only to us but, more profoundly, to God. For that reason, it is a grace that lasts and that truly liberates us for life with God. Reflect on the value of this grace as you choose how to invest your time and resources.

Because we are justified by faith, faith and obedience have to be distinguished. But their division must never destroy their unity, which lies in the reality that faith exists only in obedience, is never without obedience. Faith is only faith in deeds of obedience.

Reflection

We receive God's grace through faith but also through responding to God's call. But how do we know what God is calling us to do? God's call can come to us in the voice of other people around us, as well as through prayer, the church community, and Scripture. Obeying God's call involves paying attention to all these resources for guidance. Oftentimes, God calls us to go precisely where we would prefer not to go, even though we know doing so would be spiritually liberating. We are called to follow Jesus and obey his command, even at its most challenging. This calling is no heavy burden but instead is true freedom. Take a moment to reflect on God's calling for your life today. Where are you called to step out of your comfort zone and respond to a challenge with courage?

Day Five

In Jesus, service to the least brother or sister and service to God became one.

Reflection

Challenged to answer which commandment in the law is the greatest, Jesus responded that the greatest commandment is to love God, and the second is to love your neighbor as yourself (Matthew 22:37–40). We might worry that the commandments to love God and to love our neighbor pull us in different directions. Perhaps you are called to devote your life to a particular job or to live in a specific place but are unsure how to reconcile this with your responsibilities to your neighbors, both near and far. Or maybe your calling is to devote time and resources to serving others, but you're unsure how to balance this with providing for your children, spouse, or other friends and family members. Bonhoeffer writes that God becoming human in Jesus Christ joins together love of God and love of neighbor. By loving our neighbor we love God, who in Jesus Christ became our neighbor in the most intimate way possible. Imagine ways you can love your neighbor, confident that in doing so you are serving God.

Day Six

The time is coming when Christians, for the sake of their confession, will be excluded from "human society," as it is called, hounded from place to place, subjected to physical attack, abused, and under some circumstances even killed. The time of a widespread persecution of Christians is coming, and that is actually the real meaning of all the movements and struggles of our time. Those opponents intent upon destroying the Christian church and Christian faith cannot live together with us, because they see in all of our words and all of our actions that their own words and deeds are condemned, even if ours are not directed against them. And they are not wrong in seeing this and feeling that we are indifferent to their condemnation of us.

Bonhoeffer worked on *Discipleship* while directing an underground seminary in Finkenwalde, Germany. Under Adolf Hitler, the Nazis had sought to co-opt the church into supporting the Nazi ideology. Christians who refused to allow the church to be manipulated in this way formed the Confessing Church. The seminary Bonhoeffer led at Finkenwalde educated pastors for service in the Confessing Church. The book reflects the ideas he shared with the seminarians during that challenging time.

Reflection

Bonhoeffer reflects here on the challenge facing the church under Nazism. There was enormous pressure on the seminarians at Finkenwalde to support the Nazi government—for their own safety, for their livelihood, and for the well-being of their families. Bonhoeffer warns his readers in Nazi Germany to prepare for even more difficult times to come. Our faith today is put to the test in more everyday situations, where we might give up our basic principles and convictions when relationships, a job, or money is at stake. Where have you cast a blind eye at an injustice out of fear that speaking out carries risks that you would rather avoid? We cannot all be like Bonhoeffer, but we can learn from and seek to emulate his courage—a courage deeply grounded in his faith in God. Think of one area in your life where you can bring your actions more in line with what you believe.

Abuse of earthly goods consists in using them as a security for the next day. Worry is always directed toward tomorrow. But the goods are intended only for today in the strictest sense. It is our securing things for tomorrow which makes us so insecure today. It is enough that each day should have its own troubles. Only those who put tomorrow completely into God's hand and receive fully today what they need for their lives are really secure.

Reflection

How much of our daily lives do we spend worrying? When we are not ruminating on what happened yesterday, or last week, or ten years ago, we squander our precious time worrying about tomorrow, or the day after tomorrow. Bonhoeffer and his seminarians had plenty to worry about, trying to maintain their faith and livelihoods under Nazi hostility. Yet Bonhoeffer reminds his readers—and perhaps himself—that tomorrow is in God's hands. True security is found in accepting God's goodness today, even in this very moment. For what else do we have besides this moment? We cannot change the past, nor can we act in the future. We can act now and influence the future, but we cannot be certain how events will pan out. We lose the opportunity to live into a better future when we waste the present in worry. Focus on one worry that is occupying your mind. Imagine what it would look like to give that worry over to God in faith, knowing that the future is in God's hands.

Where the world denies justice, Christians will practice compassion; where it hides behind lies, they will speak out for those who cannot speak, and testify for the truth. For the sake of brothers or sisters—be they Jew or Greek, slave or free, strong or weak, of noble or of common birth—Christians will renounce all community with the world, for they serve the community of the body of Jesus Christ. Being a part of this community, Christians cannot remain hidden from the world. They have been called out of the world and follow Christ.

Reflection

Bonhoeffer reminds his readers that Christians are called out into the world. In Nazi Germany, he proclaimed that anti-Semitism of any kind is at odds with Scripture and with the Christian faith. In the face of racism and oppression, there is no way for the church to be neutral, no way for Christians to avoid taking a political stand. The church involves itself in the world not by providing religious commentary on the 24/7 news cycle but instead by taking up space in the world with compassion and truth. When the government ceases to protect its citizens, Christians cannot remain silent. Christians don't have to agree on every political question in order to live together as the body of Christ. By taking up space in the world and speaking for those who cannot, Christians can offer a moral alternative to injustice. Participate in the creation of this space in the world by choosing to practice truth and compassion.

The community of saints is not the "ideal" church-community of the sinless and the perfect. It is not the church-community of those without blemish, which no longer provides room for the sinner to repent. Rather it is the church-community that shows itself worthy of the gospel of the forgiveness of sins by truly proclaiming God's forgiveness, which has nothing to do with forgiving oneself. It is the community of those who have truly experienced God's costly grace, and who thereby live a life worthy of the gospel which they neither squander nor discard.

Reflection

We are often very aware of our own failings and weaknesses. It's easy to feel embarrassed and ashamed of our mistakes and to hide them from those around us. From inside and outside, we feel pressure to be spiritually and morally without blemish, not to mention successful in our careers and relationships. Bonhoeffer reminds us, however, that the church is made up of people who have understood and experienced God's costly grace. The church is not merely a building or an institution; nor is it made up of especially good, pious, or perfect people. The Christian faith is for sinners, for those who need God's forgiveness. Having experienced God's costly grace, Christians seek a life worthy of the gospel, following Jesus as disciples in word and in deed. Following Christ involves being honest with ourselves and with others about our shortcomings, our failures, our weaknesses. Only then are we prepared to follow Jesus as disciples. Consider how you can be more honest with others about your own fears, failures, and shortcomings, and witness the liberation this vulnerability can bring.

Day Ten

"Thy kingdom come"—this is not the prayer of the pious soul of the individual who wants to flee the world, nor is it the prayer of the utopian and fanatic, the stubborn world reformer. Rather, this is the prayer only of the church-community of children of the Earth, who do not set themselves apart, who have no special proposals for reforming the world to offer, who are no better than the world, but who persevere together in the midst of the world, in its depths, in the daily life and subjugation of the world.

The readings for the next three days come from a lecture Bonhoeffer gave in 1932 titled "Thy Kingdom Come! The Prayer of the Church-Community for God's Kingdom on Earth." Presented at a retreat for the Protestant Continuing Education Institute for Women, the lecture interprets the meaning of the petition "thy kingdom come," found in the Lord's Prayer. Bonhoeffer emphasizes that the church prays for God's kingdom to come here on earth. We should avoid the temptation to escape the earth for an otherworldly kingdom, forgetting that the kingdom that will come on earth is *God's* kingdom and not something we bring about of our own accord.

Reflection

Sometimes we feel like giving up on this world, despairing that it is beyond hope. In these moments, we pray for God's kingdom as a kind of escape to some other place, where the problems of the world are overcome. At other times, we take "thy kingdom come" to mean that it is our mission to actively build the kingdom, through all kinds of frenetic activity, political advocacy, and general acting for good. Bonhoeffer reminds us that the kingdom for which we pray is *God's* kingdom, not a kingdom of our own making or design. Bonhoeffer reminds us that our prayer is for God's kingdom *on earth*. We don't pray to escape the world, but rather pray and live as people who "persevere together" through challenges, hardships, injustices, and grief. Reflect throughout the day on the meaning of the prayer "thy kingdom come." How might this prayer begin to change your daily life as you choose to persevere and pursue God's kingdom on earth?

He who would flee from the world, seeking in the kingdom a place removed from his troubles, does not believe. Nor does the one who presumes that he must establish a worldly kingdom. Whoever evades the Earth finds not God but only another world, his own better, lovelier, more peaceful world. He finds a world beyond, to be sure, but never God's world, which is dawning in this world. Whoever evades Earth in order to find God finds only himself.

Reflection

We do not always know what we should hope for or what we should pray for. We might pray that God will grant us something we desire, but on reflection we realize that what we desire may not be all that good for us. Or we might not even be sure what we desire. As an example, Jesus instructs his disciples how to pray, giving them the Lord's Prayer. Today the Lord's Prayer continues to teach us how to pray, especially when we are struggling. People around the world join together daily to recite this prayer in countless languages, offering to God a prayer they could not have come up with on their own. We are taught to pray not so that we might flee the world and find ourselves but instead so that we will find God. Focus today on the prayer, "Thy will be done, on earth as it is in heaven." Let that prayer shape your hopes for your family, community, nation, and world.

Day Twelve

He who loves God, loves God as the Lord of the Earth as it is; he who loves the Earth, loves it as God's Earth.

Reflection

How do we connect our faith in God with our love of the world around us, with the sun on the horizon, with trees towering gloriously above us, and with life flourishing around us? Our love of created things—rivers, oceans, animals, our fellow human beings—reflects our love of God. In loving these things, we love God as their creator. And in loving God we are led to love the world around us and the many goods we encounter every day. We come to love the goods of the world not merely in themselves but *in God,* in whom our finite and limited love finds an enduring and everlasting home. Spend some time today admiring the beauty of the earth as God's creation. Pay attention to the details—the shape of a tree's leaves, ants working diligently underfoot, the great varieties of birdsong—reflecting on each as an example of God's eternal richness.

Day Thirteen

The Christian cannot simply take for granted the privilege of living among other Christians. Jesus Christ lived in the midst of his enemies. In the end all his disciples abandoned him. On the cross he was all alone, surrounded by criminals and the jeering crowds. He had come for the express purpose of bringing peace to the enemies of God. So Christians, too, belong not in the seclusion of a cloistered life but in the midst of enemies. There they find their mission, their work.

Today we turn to Bonhoeffer's widely read book *Life Together*. Growing out of his experience leading a Confessing Church seminary in Finkenwalde, the book underscores that the Christian life takes place in the church community, gathered together around the sacraments and the reading of Scripture. The almost monastic environment of the seminary was rather unusual for the Protestant pastors who studied there, but the format was grounded in Bonhoeffer's conviction that the Christian faith should be lived in community. While the seminary was eventually shut down by the Nazis, Bonhoeffer's discovery of the importance of the community of faith would endure, in his life and beyond.

Reflection

Sharing the life of faith with others is a joy and a privilege, but this community can be hard to find and to keep. During times of loneliness and separation, we are nourished by the time spent in community with others. We go out into the world, grounded in the faith and strength cultivated together. By the time Bonhoeffer wrote *Life Together*, the seminary he directed had been closed and the former seminarians, as well as Bonhoeffer, scattered around the country. Many of the seminarians would later perish as soldiers in the Second World War. For Bonhoeffer, it was important to remember that despite the importance of life together, Christians are not called to a cloistered life separated from the world. Instead, Christians belong among their enemies and in challenging circumstances, where they find their mission. Think about ways you can live out your faith, both in community with other Christians and in the world beyond. How might you find others to help encourage you in faith as you live and work in your world?

Day Fourteen

God has willed that we should seek and find God's living Word in the testimony of other Christians, in the mouths of human beings. Therefore, Christians need other Christians who speak God's Word to them. They need them again and again when they become uncertain and disheartened because, living by their own resources, they cannot help themselves without cheating themselves out of the truth.

Reflection

God is not merely a creator who sets the world in motion and then leaves it to its own devices. God is active, not least through the communication of God's word to human beings. God speaks. That doesn't mean we will hear God's word as a booming voice echoing down from the heavens, or even as a still, small voice in our ear. Oftentimes, we hear God in a more everyday fashion: through the words spoken to us by other people. In hearing the truths shared by those around us, we can encounter a message God wants us to hear. Knowing God's will and hearing God's word require listening, especially to those we are most inclined to ignore. It requires being attentive to truths that we would rather not hear, truths that go against our self-interest or our vanity or our preconceived notions. Spend the day listening for words you would rather not hear spoken by people you would rather ignore. Allow this deep listening to transform your life.

Day Fifteen

Those who love their dream of a Christian community more than the Christian community itself become destroyers of that Christian community even though their personal intentions may be ever so honest, earnest, and sacrificial.

Reflection

We can get caught up in visions of what a perfect community would look like, but actual human beings tend not to pair very well with idealistic visions. While Bonhoeffer has much to say about life in Christian community, he observes that more important than any ideal of community is the need simply to love and care for the people around us. When we recognize the individuality of each human being, we have to choose between either forcing the people we encounter into our model of community or paying attention to the real needs and desires of our neighbors. The trust we create through care for our neighbors as they are, not as we wish them to be, is the very essence of true community. Anything else is an illusion, which destroys trust and weakens the community. Think of an area of life where your ideal of a "perfect" community or relationship has interfered with your ability to care for your neighbors. Imagine letting go of this ideal in favor of attending to the real people around you.

As only Christ was able to speak to me in such a way that I was helped, so others too can only be helped by Christ alone. However, this means that I must release others from all my attempts to control, coerce, and dominate them with my love. In their freedom from me, other persons want to be loved for who they are, as those for whom Christ became a human being, died, and rose again, as those for whom Christ won the forgiveness of sins and prepared eternal life. Because Christ has long since acted decisively for other Christians, before I could begin to act, I must allow them the freedom to be Christ's. They should encounter me only as the persons that they already are for Christ. This is the meaning of the claim that we can encounter others only through the mediation of Christ. Self-centered love constructs its own image of other persons, about what they are and what they should become. It takes the life of the other person into its own hands. Spiritual love recognizes the true image of the other person as seen from the perspective of Jesus Christ. It is the image Jesus Christ has formed and wants to form in all people.

Reflection

Many of us have experienced moments when an act of care feels like it comes with strings attached. We feel we are in another's debt, will be constantly reminded of their help, or are made to feel guilty for their act of sacrifice. Bonhoeffer points to a love free of manipulation, a love grounded in the love of Christ. To love the neighbor in Christ is see the neighbor as they truly are. In looking at our neighbor through Christ, we can act out of love, free of all attempts to control, dominate, or save our neighbor. Paradoxically, this means that we can give ourselves more freely to our neighbors, perhaps even giving everything we have—without the burden of being our neighbor's savior. Our neighbor is free as well, able to receive our love and care without being controlled or feeling guilt. Throughout the day, remember that the people you encounter are those for whom Christ became human, died, and rose again. Let that thought transform your everyday interactions into generous acts of love.

The exclusion of the weak and insignificant, the seemingly useless people, from everyday Christian life in community *[Lebensgemeinschaft]* may actually mean the exclusion of Christ; for in the poor sister or brother, Christ is knocking at the door.

Reflection

Just as what we do for the least of these, we do for Christ, that which we do *not* do to meet the needs of people around us, we do *not* do for Christ. Bonhoeffer contrasts Jesus's teaching with a political system built around the oppression of those deemed outsiders. The Nazi regime sought to exclude Jews, as well as other minority groups, from society and pressured the church to do the same. Bonhoeffer warned that for the church to acquiesce was not merely for it to engage in injustice; it was to exclude Christ himself from the community. Where do you see the exclusion of "insignificant" people or "nonpersons" taking place in your world? How can we counteract our human tendency to set up boundaries and groups of insiders and outsiders? Reflect on how we can see Christ in the face of the excluded person and, more importantly, in the faces of those we ourselves have excluded from our lives.

Day Eighteen

Why do Christians sing when they are together? The reason is, quite simply, that in singing together it is possible for them to speak and pray the same Word at the same time—in other words, for the sake of uniting in the Word. All daily worship, all human concentration should be focused on the Word in the hymn. The fact that we do not speak it in unison, but sing it, only expresses the fact that our spoken words are inadequate to express what we want to say, that the object of our singing reaches far beyond all human words. Nevertheless, we do not mumble unintelligible words; rather we sing words of praise to God, words of thanksgiving, confession, and prayer.

Reflection

Sometimes we are comfortable singing a statement that we would be embarrassed to utter in the spoken word. Singing, and especially singing in unison with others, brings us into a different, meditative space, as our sung prayer is borne aloft to the heavens, like the voices of a magnificent choir expanding to the uppermost reaches of a towering cathedral. A musician from childhood, Bonhoeffer cherished the singing of hymns. Imagine him with his group of seminarians in the German hinterland, living in simple accommodations, gathering daily to read Scripture, break bread in Communion, and offer hymns of praise to God. During those difficult times, the seminarians came to see the power of music to strengthen communal ties. Singing in unison, the gathered people of faith make the community more real. They pray together as one voice comprised of many voices. Think of a song that is especially meaningful to you and imagine how singing it with others could bring it to life and form a bond.

The breaking of bread together has a festive quality. In the midst of the working day given to us again and again, it is a reminder that God rested after God's work, and that the Sabbath is the meaning and the goal of the week with its toil. Our life is not only a great deal of trouble and hard work; it is also refreshment and joy in God's goodness. We labor, but God nourishes and sustains us. That is a reason to celebrate.

Reflection

Eating with each other matters. We mark important rites of passage with special meals, we hold business meetings over lunch, we celebrate high holy days with elaborate festivals of food. These shared meals exhibit a kind of sacramental quality. For Bonhoeffer, life in community is itself a kind of sacrament, a sacred symbol that makes real and present the grace of Christ among us. Few of us will find ourselves in a setting like Finkenwalde, but we can become more aware of the special, sacramental quality of our shared life with family and friends. Not only during holidays and festivals, but also during an everyday meal shared with others, the breaking of bread together can serve as a sign of thanks and praise to God for the gift of community. Next time you share a meal with someone, step back, notice what makes this shared meal special, and celebrate the gift of gathering together.

Prayer offered in early morning is decisive for the day. The wasted time we are ashamed of, the temptations we succumb to, the weakness and discouragement in our work, the disorder and lack of discipline in our thinking and in our dealings with other people—all these very frequently have their cause in our neglect of morning prayer. The ordering and scheduling of our time will become more secure when it comes from prayer. The temptations of the working day will be overcome by this breakthrough to God. The decisions that are demanded by our work will become simpler and easier when they are made not in fear of other people, but solely before the face of God.

Reflection

So much of our time is wasted by the ever-present distractions of email, social media, and various other forms of electronic junk food pumped into our brains by our devices. It can seem impossible to find time for quiet reflection, but as Bonhoeffer says, a daily practice of prayer can be decisive in warding off the disorder and discouragement that plague our lives. Many of Bonhoeffer's greatest writings were composed amid chaotic circumstances hardly conducive to concentration. His activity in the church and in the political sphere could have caused him to give up theological reflection, but his dedication to daily prayer and the reading of Scripture helped him maintain focus amid the tumult of the world around him. Bonhoeffer reminds us that daily time for prayer and reflection gives us the strength and openness to go back into the world and be fully present to those we encounter. Rather than sheltering us from the world, solitude can make us more open to it. Find time today, even just five minutes, for quiet reflection away from the internet, phones, and other distractions.

Day Twenty-One

Only in the community do we learn to be properly alone; and only in being alone do we learn to live properly in the community. It is not as if the one preceded the other; rather both begin at the same time, namely, with the call of Jesus Christ. Each taken by itself has profound pitfalls and perils. Those who want community without solitude plunge into the void of words and feelings, and those who seek solitude without community perish in the bottomless pit of vanity, self-infatuation, and despair. Whoever cannot be alone should beware of community. Whoever cannot stand being in community should beware of being alone.

Reflection

Perhaps you long to go home and be alone at the end of each day, sheltered from the challenges, noise, and people around you. Or perhaps you feel a kind of insatiable restlessness, always needing to hurry from here to there in conversation and community with others. Whether you crave time to yourself or ceaseless activity with other human beings, Bonhoeffer warns that both solitude and community can be dangerous when they are not held in balance. If we are unable to be alone, the opportunity for community is not a joyful gift but rather a defense against fear. If we unable to be in community, solitude becomes a strategy to avoid the stress of other people instead of a gift from God. Bonhoeffer encourages us to accept *both* solitude and community as divine gifts and to nourish both in our everyday lives. Reflect on how you balance time alone and time spent among others and accept the challenge of seeking out both solitude and community.

Day Twenty-Two

The first service one owes to others in the community involves listening to them. Just as our love for God begins with listening to God's Word, the beginning of love for other Christians is learning to listen to them. God's love for us is shown by the fact that God not only gives us God's Word, but also lends us God's ear. We do God's work for our brothers and sisters when we learn to listen to them.

Reflection

The capacity to listen to one another sounds straightforward and yet can be incredibly difficult. There is so much happening, so many people talking, texting, tweeting, and blogging, that it can be hard to hear the friend or loved one right in front of us. A close friend is speaking to us while we scroll through a never-ending Facebook newsfeed, "listening" to the voices of distant acquaintances we hardly know and ultimately aren't that interested in knowing. Yet we hand over our precious attention, the finite minutes and hours that make up our lives, failing to listen to those who really deserve our attention. The good news is that we can learn to listen again, to put away our distractions and listen in the way that God listens to us: with love. The next time someone important to you is talking, try listening with all your attention. Put down your phone, set aside your own ideas, and listen attentively to what they are saying.

The service of forgiveness is done by one to the other on a daily basis. It occurs without words in intercessory prayer for one another. And all members of the community who do not grow tired of doing this service can depend on the fact that this service is also being offered to them by other Christians. Those who bear with others know that they themselves are being borne. Only in this strength can they themselves bear with others.

Reflection

We often think of forgiveness as a one-time event: someone wrongs us, we muster the courage to forgive them, and the story ends. But according to Bonhoeffer, forgiveness is a recurring, daily practice that goes both ways. We need to forgive others and recognize our own need to be forgiven, even when we don't feel especially in need of forgiveness or especially called to forgive others. Sometimes we might not know what we've done wrong and yet need forgiveness nevertheless. At other times we need to forgive those who are unaware of how they've hurt us. Bonhoeffer reminds us that our life together requires that we daily seek forgiveness for the wrongs we have done to others and forgive those who have hurt us. Think of someone who has wronged you and consider what it would look like to forgive them, remembering that you rely on others to forgive you.

One who because of sensitivity and vanity rejects the serious words of another Christian cannot speak the truth in humility to others. Such a person is afraid of being rejected and feeling hurt by another's words. Sensitive, irritable people will always become flatterers, and very soon they will come to despise and slander other Christians in their community. But humble people will cling to both truth and love. They will stick to the Word of God and let it lead them to others in their community. They can help others through the Word because they seek nothing for themselves and have no fears for themselves.

Reflection

Sometimes we're afraid to tell friends something we know they don't want to hear, and other times words spoken to us by a friend, however true, sting and cause us pain. Bonhoeffer reminds us that failure to love and disdain for the truth go hand in hand. When we are overcome by pride and fear of rejection, we cannot tolerate the truth and we become unable to love. In such moments, we are more likely to avoid hard conversations than to act in the calm courage required to tell and hear the truth. But perfect love drives out the fear that makes us hostile to the truth. When we act out of humility, we love for the sake of truth and tell the truth for the sake of love. This requires courage, since telling the truth in love invites conflict, resistance, and listening to challenging words about ourselves. Remember that "perfect love casts out fear" (1 John 4:18). Reflect on this verse throughout the day and allow God's love to give you the courage to embrace truth.

In confession there takes place a breakthrough to community. Sin wants to be alone with people. It takes them away from the community. The more lonely people become, the more destructive the power of sin over them. The more deeply they become entangled in it, the more unholy is their loneliness. Sin wants to remain unknown. It shuns the light. In the darkness of what is left unsaid sin poisons the whole being of a person. This can happen in the midst of a pious community. In confession the light of the gospel breaks into the darkness and closed isolation of the heart.

Reflection

We tend to put on a bright, happy face in public, keeping our dark side hidden from others. As Bonhoeffer says, "sin wants to remain unknown." Out of fear and shame, we hide our weaknesses from those around us. While it seems easier to share only our best selves, this practice leads to loneliness and isolation. Bonhoeffer sought to restore the ancient Christian practice of confession, in which we openly share our failures and mistakes with others. The practice of confession can break this cycle of isolation and fear, opening up space for our weaknesses to see the light of day. This was a profoundly countercultural act in Bonhoeffer's time, just as it would be today. Opening up about our shortcomings is a risky endeavor, but the risk allows for the reward of reconciling broken relationships. Think of things you tend to keep to yourself and consider how these secrets lead to loneliness. Imagine how admitting your weaknesses to another might change and strengthen your relationships.

Day Twenty-Six

Because time is the most precious gift at our disposal, being of all gifts the most irretrievable, the thought of time possibly lost disturbs us whenever we look back. Time is lost when we have not lived, experienced things, learned, worked, enjoyed, and suffered as human beings. Lost time is unfulfilled, empty time. Certainly that is not what the past years have been. We have lost much, things far beyond measure, but time was not lost. Indeed, the insights and experiences we have gained and of which we have subsequently become aware are only abstractions from reality, from life itself. Yet just as the ability to forget is a gift of grace, so similarly is memory, the repetition of received teachings, part of responsible life.

At the end of the year 1942, Bonhoeffer circulated a reflective essay among his close associates involved in a conspiracy against Adolf Hitler. Titled "After Ten Years," the essay reflects on the experience of living in Germany under Nazi control since 1933. Bonhoeffer wrote the essay only a few months before he was arrested and imprisoned, and it is published as an introduction to Bonhoeffer's *Letter's and Papers from Prison*. The passages for the next three days come from this essay.

Reflection

All of us regret choices we have made in the past. Thinking that we have wasted precious time or reflecting on what we didn't accomplish can overwhelm us with grief. Bonhoeffer was in a good position to think about lost time. His entire life trajectory was thrown off course by the rise of the Nazi regime in 1933. Although he was a prolific writer who once held a university position in Berlin, by the time he composed this essay he had been forbidden to publish his writings or even to speak in public. Instead of lamenting wasted years, he reflects on what it would mean to lose time and realizes that he has not done so at all. Memory gives meaning to the events of our lives, so that even hard times come to be understood as part of a larger story. We might even look back on difficult events in life and mistakes we have made with a strange kind of gratitude, as we come to interpret these events as part of the story of how we became who we are. Think back on various events in your life up until now. How have these experiences shaped the person you have become?

Day Twenty-Seven

Have there ever been people in history who in their time, like us, had so little ground under their feet, people to whom every possible alternative open to them at the time appeared equally unbearable, senseless, and contrary to life? Have there been those who like us looked for the source of their strength beyond all those available alternatives? Were they looking entirely in what has passed away and in what is yet to come? And nevertheless, without being dreamers, did they await with calm and confidence the successful outcome of their endeavor? Or rather, facing a great historical turning point, and precisely because something genuinely new was coming to be that did not fit with the existing alternatives, did the responsible thinkers of another generation ever feel differently than we do today?

Reflection

Addressing his fellow conspirators against Hitler and the Nazis, Bonhoeffer reflects on how their lives have changed over the past ten years. Much of what they had known and held dear was lost. It appeared that their country would soon be destroyed. We can understand why Bonhoeffer says that the very ground under their feet had collapsed. Even in less dramatic circumstances, we can experience a shaking of the foundations of our lives. Despite our best efforts, events beyond our control can wreak havoc on us. This was the case for Bonhoeffer, and yet in the midst of the chaos around him he avoided despair. In our own lives it could well be political and social forces that wreck our best laid plans. Or it could be disease, a broken marriage, or the loss of a job that sends our lives spiraling out of control. When the ground beneath us begins to shake, we remember that God is our firm foundation.

It remains an experience of incomparable value that we have for once learned to see the great events of world history from below, from the perspective of the outcasts, the suspects, the maltreated, the powerless, the oppressed and reviled, in short from the perspective of the suffering. If only during this time bitterness and envy have not corroded the heart; that we come to see matters great and small, happiness and misfortune, strength and weakness with new eyes; that our sense for greatness, humanness, justice, and mercy has grown clearer, freer, more incorruptible; that we learn, indeed, that personal suffering is a more useful key, a more fruitful principle than personal happiness for exploring the meaning of the world in contemplation and action. But this perspective from below must not lead us to become advocates for those who are perpetually dissatisfied. Rather, out of a higher satisfaction, which in its essence is grounded beyond what is below and above, we do justice to life in all its dimensions and in this way affirm it.

Reflection

Most of us have had the experience of simply not seeing something because it was outside of our area of concern or because it was in our interest *not* to see it. In our better moments, we acknowledge that our own bias and self-interest lead us to notice only what we want to notice. Bonhoeffer encourages us to observe the great events of history "from below." We fail to perceive the world as it actually is unless we are willing to look at it from below. We need to pay special attention to the poor, the weak, the powerless. This is not merely a moral admonition. What might seem like a reasonable policy, or at most a necessary evil, comes to be seen in its full brutality through the perspective of the suffering. Reflect on how considering the interests of the marginalized changes how you evaluate a particular action, proposal, or policy. How might talking to those most affected shape our thoughts and convictions?

Day Twenty-Nine

In the last few years I have come to know and understand more and more the profound this-worldliness of Christianity. The Christian is not a *homo religiosus* but simply a human being, in the same way that Jesus was a human being—in contrast, perhaps, to John the Baptist. I do not mean the shallow and banal this-worldliness of the enlightened, the bustling, the comfortable, or the lascivious, but the profound this-worldliness that shows discipline and includes the ever-present knowledge of death and resurrection.

In April 1943, Bonhoeffer was arrested and imprisoned at Tegel military prison in Berlin. He would remain in prison for what would be the final two years of his life. During this time, Bonhoeffer continued his theological writings, primarily in the form of letters written to his close friend Eberhard Bethge. In April 1945, Bonhoeffer was executed at Flossenbürg concentration camp, only two weeks before the camp was liberated by US forces. After Bonhoeffer's death, Bethge collected Bonhoeffer's prison writings and published them as *Letters and Papers from Prison.*

Reflection

During the most difficult times in life, we are tempted to give up hope on this world, marred as it is by suffering, disease, injustice, and cruelty. We might even give in to despair and become unable to hope for change. Imprisoned by a brutal regime, Bonhoeffer began to reflect more deeply on what he called the "this-worldliness" of Christian faith, on what faith means for how we live and experience the everyday realities of ordinary life. Faith calls us to live this life to its full potential, aware of the unique opportunity we are given between birth and death, and in hope of the resurrection. When we are fully present, we avoid the temptation to squander God's gift of life. Reflect today on how faith enlivens and deepens your experience of day-to-day life.

Day Thirty

I thought I myself could learn to have faith by trying to live something like a saintly life. I suppose I wrote *Discipleship* at the end of this path. Today I clearly see the dangers of that book, though I still stand by it. Later on I discovered, and am still discovering to this day, that one only learns to have faith by living in the full this-worldliness of life. If one has completely renounced making something of oneself—whether it be a saint or a converted sinner or a church leader (a so-called priestly figure!), a just or an unjust person, a sick or a healthy person—then one throws oneself completely into the arms of God, and this is what I call this-worldliness: living fully in the midst of life's tasks, questions, successes and failures, experiences, and perplexities—then one takes seriously no longer one's own sufferings but rather the suffering of God in the world.

Reflection

Sometimes we hope that faith will solve all our problems, answer all our questions, cure us of all doubts. We think everything will finally make sense, if only we just believe. But things are rarely so simple. To throw oneself completely into the arms of God, as Bonhoeffer puts it, does not mean that everything will suddenly make perfect sense or that all our problems will be solved. Instead, faith asks us to accept that life includes not only successes but also failures, not only answers but also questions and riddles that will never be resolved. Trapped in a Nazi prison, Bonhoeffer came to see what it means to live a life of faith: to give one's life fully to God, wherever God calls. Shortly before he was marched to his execution at Flossenbürg concentration camp, Bonhoeffer reportedly said, "This is the end—for me the beginning of life." This world is only a taste—but a taste nonetheless—of the new creation that God has begun in Jesus Christ. Take a moment to be grateful not only for success but also for failure, not only for answers but also for questions. Consider how all of these things are gifts from God.

Further Reading

Bethge, Eberhard. *Dietrich Bonhoeffer: A Biography*. Edited by Victoria J. Barnett. Rev. ed. Minneapolis: Fortress Press, 2000.

Bonhoeffer, Dietrich. *Dietrich Bonhoeffer Works*. 17 vols. Minneapolis: Fortress Press, 1996–2014.

DeJonge, Michael P. *Bonhoeffer's Theological Formation: Berlin, Barth, and Protestant Theology*. Oxford: Oxford University Press, 2012.

Green, Clifford J. *Bonhoeffer: A Theology of Sociality*. Rev. ed. Grand Rapids: Eerdmans, 1999.

Lovin, Robin W. *Christian Faith and Public Choices: The Social Ethics of Barth, Brunner, and Bonhoeffer*. Philadelphia: Fortress Press, 1984.

Rasmussen, Larry L. *Dietrich Bonhoeffer: Reality and Resistance*. Louisville: Westminster John Knox, 2005.

Sifton, Elisabeth, and Fritz Stern. *No Ordinary Men: Dietrich Bonhoeffer and Hans von Dohnanyi, Resisters against Hitler in Church and State*. New York: New York Review Books, 2013.

Tietz, Christiane. *Theologian of Resistance: The Life and Thought of Dietrich Bonhoeffer*. Translated by Victoria J. Barnett. Minneapolis: Fortress Press, 2016.

Passages

The passages in this book are all taken from Dietrich Bonhoeffer, *Dietrich Bonhoeffer Works*, 17 vols. (Minneapolis: Fortress Press, 1996–2014), cited below as DBW.

Day 1: DBW 4:51

Day 2: DBW 4:44

Day 3: DBW 4:45

Day 4: DBW 4:64

Day 5: DBW 4:124

Day 6: DBW 4:142

Day 7: DBW 4:165

Day 8: DBW 4:237

Day 9: DBW 4:269

Day 10: DBW 12:290

Day 11: DBW 12:288

Day 12: DBW 12:288

Day 13: DBW 5:27

Day 14: DBW 5:32

Day 15: DBW 5:36

Day 16: DBW 5:43–44

Day 17: DBW 5:45–46

Day 18: DBW 5:66

Day 19: DBW 5:73

Day 20: DBW 5:76

Day 21: DBW 5:83

Day 22: DBW 5:98

Day 23: DBW 5:103

Day 24: DBW 5:105

Day 25: DBW 5:110

Day 26: DBW 8:37

Day 27: DBW 8:38

Day 28: DBW 8:52

Day 29: DBW 8:485

Day 30: DBW 8:486